Journey to Within

*One Woman's Glimpse
into the Living Peace Code*

By

Emma Porter

"Chakra Dance" cover art created by Ben Gill © 2016.

Dedication

I dedicate this book to all individuals in the world who grapple with any form of addiction, low self worth, and who either hide their struggles or can't find the courage to share with someone for constructive assistance.

It is okay to not feel okay, it is also okay to take a pause and begin to step through struggle to relearn a new way of thought and living. Everyone is worth a way of living that empowers each soul and embodies peace.

Acknowledgements

It is with deep gratitude and immense joy that I am able to take this moment to acknowledge some deep connections along my journey.

I wish to acknowledge my parents, Margaret and Andrew Shute, for your love and commitment to raising me, especially since I recognize I may not have been an easy child/teenager to bring up! I love that your present work continues to be in service to others, whether as Deacon for the Catholic Church (Dad) or Hospital Chaplain (Mum).

To my extended family members for all their love, support and laughter, I thank you.

I would like to acknowledge Richard Porter, to thank you for saying "Yes" to our twenty years, our worldwide adventures together. Thank you, Richard, for our beautiful sons, memories created and for showing courage and integrity in your decision making regarding our family.

Thank you, Nicholas (Nick) Porter. At this time we are entering a time of intense growth together. I thank you for your brilliant sense of humor, bear hugs and being my personal teacher regarding the teen years. I love your Spirit!

Jonathan Porter, I thank you for seeing the light in those you meet. For being an eight-year-old who is sensitive, sweet and organized. I love your Spirit!

I also want to acknowledge you, my mentor, Alaric Hutchinson, founder of Earth Spirit Center for Healing for the incredible training program and mentoring, for our growth together as teacher and student, for your trust in me, for all the opportunities given, and for asking me to write this book. What a process! I am thrilled to think of the future journeys I, myself, and others will have using the *Living Peace*/Dunisha approach!

I want to acknowledge Maria Cooke for being one of five core people in my life and sharing your extensive knowledge in energy work with me. Thank you for your unwavering faith in my ability, even when I myself could not see it.

I want to acknowledge the community of Earth Spirit Center for Healing/The Dunisha Sanctuary, both members who were there from its first opening or those who became members after the reopening of the center. I am grateful for all that was shared with me through courage and vulnerability, for the support and love given and those rich, deep connections. The community, at all stages, has taught me so very much and given me beautiful memories I'll always cherish.

I want to acknowledge Aaron, Chaske, Chris, Derrick (yes, I hear you "Big Bro") Paul and Ricardo for demonstrating that strong bonds of friendship can be created and developed and can transcend difficult situations—even death. Thank each and every one of you for all the sharing and laughter via penmanship.

I want to acknowledge Mark, for your solid confidence in me and my solar plexus chakra, your steady, unwavering support and for being a witness to my process.

I want to acknowledge Ellorien for our enjoyable telephone conversations, your encouragement, and for reminding me, when I needed it, to be in touch with who I am!

Late June, 2016, Ellorien passed away, "Spring Lea" thank you for being inspirational and amazing to so many people!

I want to acknowledge Elizabeth Anne Hill for embodying important messages I deeply appreciate (since you travel globally) and for your inspiration.

I want to thank you, my brilliant, extremely patient editor, Shari Broyer, for working through the collision of my British and American spellings and grammar and the "what do you really mean" moments! I've learned a tremendous amount through your editing. I truly appreciate your input in this process of writing.

Allen Daley, not all angels are found in heaven; thank you for walking the earth.

To a special little girl, my god-daughter, Courtney Skuse: Though we live in different countries, I will always do my best to be there for you. May you never forget the "shiny light" within you.

I would like to thank a man, known simply as "El" for planting in me the seed—all those years ago in Singapore—that grew into the path I then found after coming to Arizona.

I could continue on forever as I truly am thankful to everyone for the connections made—past, present or future—and to Spirit for the gifts of Life, Peace, Love and Immense Joy!

Foreword

By Alaric Hutchinson

Dunshia Emma, the Compassionate

I first met Emma Porter back in 2011 when I was pastor of church services at Earth Spirit Center for Healing. She began attending, and it wasn't long before she took on teaching Sunday school. Through the ebb and flow of the church experience for two years, I witnessed just how patient and thoughtfully responsible Emma was. In time, I decided to change spiritual directions and guide others to inner peace as a Dunisha Monk rather than shepherd a congregation as a pastor. It was my greatest pleasure when Emma became one of the first enrollees in my Dunisha Healing™ Program. I knew she would flourish, and she did.

Emma has walked alongside me since the inception of Dunisha Healing ™ and has watched my *Living Peace* teachings start out as the seeds of an idea, take root as daily lifestyles, and become the beautiful blossoming garden they are today—bringing insight and serenity to people all over the world. Since the beginning, Emma has been a strong believer in the ideals of *Living Peace* and Dunisha, and it is such a humble privilege and joy that my book inspired her to write her own book to share her unique approach to the lessons contained within the Living Peace Code.

Journey to Within retains the essence of *Living Peace* while taking on a life of its own as Emma recounts her magnificent path to learning and applying these powerful teachings. Her "journey to within" is an exciting and transformative experience that I am certain every reader will benefit from and enjoy.

"Dunisha" is the peaceful, healing way of Earth and Spirit, and "Dunshia"—or "Dunshio", as the masculine version—references one who has been ordained as a Dunisha Monk. On the way to becoming a Dunshia, Emma has undergone a tremendous metamorphosis, receiving guidance, not only from me, but from life itself.

Every day is a miracle and every day offers new experiences to learn form. As Dunisha Masters, we have taken vows to promote mindfulness and peace, proactively applying the Living Peace Code to our daily lives. The cultivation of inner peace is an ever-expanding journey, one with many tools to choose from as we tend and grow our own gardens; however, the pages in Emma's book will surely offer some wisdom to any person seeking to live life with greater inner harmony and outward compassion for the others we are blessed to walk with on this magnificent planet.

In peace,

Alaric Hutchinson

Dunshio and Author of *Living Peace*

Table of Contents

The Living Peace Code

P.E.A.C.E.
People **E**mbracing **A** **C**onscious **E**volution

I **AM** the Master of my Life:
I Master my Thoughts.
I Master my Impulses.
I Master my Emotions.

I see **THROUGH** Illusion:
There is no Ignorance.
There is no Chaos.
There is no Duality.

I Forever **SEEK** and Cultivate:
Understanding,
Harmony, and,
Transcendence.

Everything is Impermanent. Change is the only Constant.

I RELEASE my Attachments to the Mundane World.
I RELEASE my Attachments to What I Know.
I RELEASE my Attachments to Who I Am.
I RELINQUISH... **My SELF**...

I **AM**
P.E.A.C.E.
People **E**mbodying **A** **C**onscious **E**volution

Alaric Hutchinson, author
Excerpted from his book, *Living Peace*

My Introduction to the Living Peace Code

Each Sunday during our Circle of Peace at Earth Spirit Center for Healing, we like to bring our attention to the beginning of the Living Peace Code by "embracing" peace and conclude with the idea of "embodying" peace. This is of great value because starting with embracing leads to an openness—a "teachability", if you will—that makes room for transformation to occur. Once we have embraced a state of peace, the embodiment of peace can follow, which is potent because embodying something then gives it the power to affect the mind and body, thus altering our experienced reality.

Meditation and mindfulness literally have been proven to change the brain. For example, in 2011, a team led by Sara Lazar at Harvard University discovered that the structure of the brain was changed due to mindfulness meditation. Cortical thickness in the hippocampus *increased*. This area of the brain oversees memory and learning and has a part in the regulation of emotions. Additionally, brain cell volume *decreased* in the amygdala, the primal part of the brain linked to fear, stress and anxiety. The changes reported matched the participants' feedback regarding the lessening of their own stress levels. Changes in the brain linked to mood and meditation matched improvements in the wellbeing of the participants.

I often say to my friends that it would have been fascinating to have had a brain scan prior to my study of *Living Peace* and the Dunisha Healing™ Program and contrast it with the results at the end of 2015 after my completion of this book and ordination as a master!

I remember the moment I chose to embrace this code that I now live my life by. The Living Peace Code had been recently produced as a poster, framed and displayed on the sanctuary wall after the reopening of the center in the summer of 2014. I had some understanding of how "Chaos is an Illusion" due to attending on previous Sundays, but I still felt wishy-washy about the concept. I then sat and reflected for a considerable time on the poster as a whole, so much so that memorization of it became second nature. The more I meditated on the words, they resonated with me, and I felt a deeper sense of inner peace stir within my soul.

Each Sunday during our Circle of Peace we, as a community, encourage each other to ask questions, and to bring in and share various texts, experiences, and stories. I felt then and there that the intention of these words penned by Alaric Hutchinson were pure and made sense to me. Peace *is* a foundation for experiencing love and joy and being authentic! So often, people look externally for peace, love, happiness and bypass the crucial stage of finding it first within themselves.

I thought, "I am going to be open and go with this, because I feel very much guided to do so for my self growth." I feel it's amazing that I am now writing this book and sharing stories of what led me to my own moments of healing and self-actualization. I look upon my life as a journey filled with adventure, but I had no idea that this code would soon take me on a vibrant, internal and external, ongoing, dedicated adventure, one that I could not have even begun to imagine the day I first walked through the Center doors and met Alaric.

It is my joy to share my story. May the Living Peace Code and the words within these pages inspire self-reflection in you, my readers, as they have so often done in me. Take what you will and leave the rest—there is no expectation.

So, it is in peace, love, compassion and joy that I share the words upon these pages,

Emma

Everyone is worthy of feeling good, everyone is worthy of being heard and supported, everyone is worthy of finding their own balance and boundaries. Creation begins with thought and what a brilliant way to begin by investing in oneself! Thus, let us begin with the mantra that my teacher, Alaric Hutchinson, so often had me reiterate, "I Am the Master of My Life."

ᴄenec One

Mastery of Thought:
"I Think Peace"

"You smell!" These two little words, when put together, are words that most people do not want to hear. So, when I was told this, after a cautionary, "This is sensitive" my immediate reaction was horror.

I was mortified. My racing thoughts jumped to an old memory of struggling with encopresis (soiling associated with stool holding) with one of my children and clung to that, believing it must be the root of this unwanted observation. I wanted to go home and react in a desperate manner to fix what I was not aware of, since I believed I already knew when I might be "smelly"!

Clearly, being told I had an odor could imply thoughts of *you don't wash enough* or *you have poor hygiene*, etc. As a practitioner of the Living Peace Code, I recalled a saying that had once been shared with me: "What others think of you is none of your business." I kept this saying in my mind as my husband and I systematically approached this person's viewpoint, trying to figure out how I, and then my family, might smell to the individual. The funny thing was—a month earlier, I had nearly called off a gathering at my home in which a friend was to be a guest speaker because I was overly worried that our new pup was too "smelly"! I joked to the speaker that I was reacting from fear, since I do clean my home, but my desire to see humans connect was more important than my fear that my home smelled a tad or the pup acted too crazy!

As a practitioner, I am convinced that my training reduced my levels of stress even though, in my obsessive thinking, I went out and spent $300 on products I had already used plus some new supplies, and I also felt increased anxiety because the person had suggested I invest in a clothes dryer. Having lived in three other countries, drying clothes without a dryer has never been an issue. Asking around, only one other person reported an "on and off scent" but "not a big deal". I believed, from the body language of the others I asked, that they were being honest in their "smell not noticed" feedback. But, then, due to my training, I caught my behavior and commanded myself to stop. A two-month period of observation weighted against the years I'd known the person who told me I smelled is nothing in the grand scheme of time. Instead, I could see and value that the person—my friend, at the end of the day—had been showing compassion by informing me that I smelled.

As with all our senses, what we smell or do not smell can vary widely among people. My bruised ego had a moment of wanting to ban hugs out of courtesy and respect for all until I felt secure again. However, a short phone call with another friend reminded me we are all spiritual beings having very human issues at times. After another conversation in which I asked, "How do I fix what I am not sure I can?" and that friend suggested, "Try one variable at a time." I was able to rise above the mundane, feeling better about myself and the other person. At the time of writing this, I realize that incident was probably the greatest test of how I was progressing in the program.

Loading the washing machine with a different detergent and using the extra wash cycle for a little while cleared up the issue once I found the courage to ask. Of course, now I have a 'tween boy who comes with his own unique smells!

Perception is everything! I have chosen this example for thought, since what we think is ever-changing. Because of the initial stress I experienced, I made assumptions. These are illusions. What is experienced as "true" for one person may not be so for another person, and beliefs can be adjusted. No matter what the issue, whether we give or receive messages, how we interpret them is up to us. It takes awareness and persistence to master our thoughts and allow us to unify with others versus separate from them.

The Arts or keywords in addressing Mastery of Thought are Illusion and Belief. Are you familiar with The Boring Figure, a famous ambiguous illusion? I recommend looking it up if not. Some people will initially see the head of an old lady and others a younger woman. By changing perception, it is possible to switch between the two, and this is how I like to explain illusion, in a simple demonstration, since everything we think is perception.

The Boring Figure is a complete image, and individuals bring to it their own perception. Neither view is right or wrong though both are looking at the same thing. Perception can be shifted; it does not need to be permanent. When it comes to dealing with the world and its billions of perceptions, the Boring Figure has always led me to a sense of peace. And working more with illusion and beliefs through Living Peace and The Dunisha Sanctuary has helped me immensely.

Alaric Hutchinson shares a practice called The File Exchange (p122 Living Peace) that helps us with our thoughts. The subconscious mind (beliefs) is like the filing cabinet and the files within it are our thoughts, the conscious mind. When was the last time you went through the files (thoughts) in your filing cabinet (mind) and examined, perhaps challenged and updated, what was in there?

One evening at ESC, a fun question was asked of all. "If you could have one super power what would it be?" As people took turns answering, it struck me—I was sitting amongst super heroes!

Again, thanks to perception, the definition of what a superhero is will vary among people, but all I could see, despite their answers, was a group of people dedicated to their self development and examining their belief systems: examining, challenging, going through many layers to release unhelpful beliefs and reformatting them. This "superhero" reformat led to harmony and joy that shone from within. Beliefs are powerful! They are tools. We can use them negatively to suffer and limit, or positively to feel great, to inspire and create! It is never too late, no matter what we are told, to implement changes!

Tenet Two

Mastery of Impulse:
"I Act Peace"

Monday, August 31, 2015

It was while contemplating this chapter that I gained the joyful realization that since I first had access to the Internet many years ago, today was the first time I took an online eating disorder self test and my results came back completely counter to those I had gotten every other time I had taken one!

When I was in my 20s, sitting in a Psychology lecture, I first realized (and it hit me hard), "I have dis-ordered eating."

Because I was a student, the university I attended was able to fast track me over to a unit to receive counseling, but since it was still weeks before I was due to begin sessions, I moved country without regret.

As a reader, you may now be expecting a story to accompany the "why", the root reason I had been in a dis-ordered relationship with food since my teenage years. This is irrelevant. The point you would benefit to grasp here is that I had thoughts, impulses and emotions that were not helping me to be the healthiest I could be.

Years later, when in Asia, I walked a path that led me to a Buddhist Meditation Center. Here, I discovered my own soul's dance, and it was at this point that I began to look deeper into ways I could help myself. I began to challenge myself. I took the action of deciding to meditate regularly and worked with a hypnotherapist who assisted me in finding peace regarding some relationships in my past. He gently stirred my awareness regarding the power of belief. This was enough of a shift that I no longer felt like I was mentally on my knees and began to work myself out of the prison my mind had created and reinforced with negative thoughts.

Something I find most interesting is that within the past four years (since I began attending circle at the Center) I have become happiest with myself physically. Even though I remained heavy, I did not attach conditions to my self worth, and those around me noticed this. I became so comfortable with myself that I decided to allow my body to become an art canvas for a local body painter! The lesson I have learned is that when one sees, hears and holds oneself without judgment, change naturally occurs. I am grateful for that journey.

I master my impulses.

"This tenet encourages us to develop greater self-discipline and cultivate willpower so that we may be in better control of our impulses, which then allows us to consciously choose how we interact with life." (p52, *Living Peace*)

It is through being dedicated to working with our thoughts that we rewire our impulses and emotions. I would like to mention that Alaric Hutchinson describes ego as "one's sense of self that is separate from others", or in other words, "one's sense of self that negatively separates from others through comparisons, judgment, and criticism". Often, we tend to think of ego as an inflated sense of self, but there is also the other aspect of it, low self-esteem, and that was where I found myself residing, with its companion, self-criticism.

After the birth of my second child, I heard these words spoken regretfully by the counselor at my doctor's office, "I am sorry. There is nothing we can do." I didn't fit the classification of "excessively large" or "dangerously underweight". Private treatment for my weight gain was not an option within my available budget, so I continued doing the best I could, with what I knew, just as I had done in previous times of seeking assistance and meeting with what felt like a brick wall. By educating myself and dedicatedly applying what I learned before my move to Arizona, my belief system gradually changed to one in which I felt more empowered than out of control.

Awareness is such a blessed tool when it comes to mastering impulses. In this chapter of *Living Peace*, we also learned to PPR — Pause, Process, Respond (or Respond/Retreat/Release, whatever is most appropriate at the time.) We were taught to pause, take deep breaths, and then respond. The breath is a POWERFUL tool! Deep breathing breaks toxins up and has been proven to help the body to respond in many positive ways, from relaxing muscles, reducing stress, achieving better blood flow, to releasing endorphins and clarifying the mind. Breathing exercises assist the body with the "fight or flight" response. Deep, slow breaths inform the brain to relax by stimulating the parasympathetic reaction that can calm us down during times of extreme stress and help us feel more in control. It is natural for stress and anxiety to be present in life; however, high, constant levels of stress negatively affect our wellbeing.

The exercise of PPR helped me in particular because, through it, I became aware that my energy levels would increase — or, I would feel more relaxed — depending on which intention I held when deliberately breathing deeper! I have always considered myself a fairly patient person; still, I began to witness that some of my interactions with other people went more smoothly simply because I was aware of my breath. Some of those people, for example family members, also noticed I was responding differently!

Working on mastery of impulse also helped me tremendously during an anxious delay to see a specialist. December 11, 2015, I went in for a colonoscopy. The initial fear I experienced before I even went to see the doctor tempted me to believe that my ability to parent and my social life would be put in jeopardy, and how could this happen now, when I was in a transition to co-parenting? Part of me wanted to hibernate away; part of me questioned, "Am I going to sound like a broken record to my friends?" Then the "what if's" popped up. All I could do in that moment was sit and embrace what I felt. Fearful thoughts expressed by others meant a huge opportunity to work through their views as well as my own. At one point, it seemed a possibility that I would have to up and leave my home, returning to the UK with my children and pets within a four-week time frame in order to avoid extremely high medical bills. My mind and body wanted to just inch away from sight, but I choose the path of peace, the path to courageously seek and create a better reality for myself and my family while working with the information being provided. I wrote part of this chapter during my wait to see the doctor.

Fortunately, I was mindful of the regular commitment I had made to take care of myself and my needs, and I used PPR to take a pause and respond to my fears with, "How can I authentically help myself here?" The answers varied from tapping more into compassion, to living more in the present by taking it one day at a time, to researching a book or two that might help me with the physical pain. Also, I was able to learn different ways of using some information that I had received through Dunisha and *Living Peace* that allowed me to listen to what my body was telling me and to be honest and factual with those around me. The more I took pause and adjusted my mindset, the less stress and anxiety I felt, promoting a grounded awareness, which began to lessen the amount of pain I experienced at times.

As you can see by my example, impulses are not necessarily negative, but they do involve a strong urge to commit actions repetitively. This often results in further harm. As with mastering any skill, it takes practice and development, and, as with all the *Living Peace* tenets, it is a continuous process for me.

Tenet Three

Mastery of Emotion:
"I Am Peace"

"The path of peace is not a passive journey. It takes incredible strength not to open a can of 'whoop ass' justifiably, when one's button is pushed." – T.F. Hodge

I have chosen to share and thereby remind myself as well as you, dear reader, that peace is not passive; instead it is an active journey and process.

What I really enjoy and value about the Dunisha Sanctuary is that, although a core keystone is peace, there is tremendous freedom when it comes to individual dreams and goals. There is no timetable that passes or fails one for not achieving peace by such and such a date.

However, there have been times where I have asked myself, "Where am I, when it comes to mastering my emotions?" for when we are regularly surrounded by those we recognize as our spiritual family, it is easy to feel too comfortable and fall into routine. Routine is wonderful, but when we step out of our comfort zones, deliberately or otherwise, we can check in with where we are at in any given moment. I knew traveling to Australia for a holiday would be a fabulous opportunity to evaluate my progress toward the goals I had set for myself.

It began with our arrival in Phoenix: there was a problem with one of our three flight connections, and we had not been informed of the change. Over an hour later, my two boys and I were finally re-ticketed. During that time I had confident faith we would still be leaving for Australia that day, so it was easy to feel at peace.

When the boys and I arrived in Melbourne, we discovered the airline in Phoenix had suspended the boys' tickets to Brisbane. I had no way of contacting my husband or the airline, thanks to my cell phone carrier failing to change my phone plan to roaming as I'd requested in a call prior to the trip.

I began to feel a tear (or more) start to leak, which I recognized as tiredness, so I immediately centered myself. I gave gratitude for my amazing traveler boys, who in that moment were patient, polite and happy, so much so that this was noticed and complimented on many times by strangers.

I gave and *felt* gratitude that we'd made it to Melbourne safely, and that I was able to take some money out at a kiosk which then allowed me to send my husband and two other friends a text message. (Which, by the way, didn't arrive, I later found out, but it helped me feel better at the time.) I was not in danger, so being at peace felt effortless as we then sat around. Effortless, yet I was still antsy to get there as we waited for the airline office to open that morning.

Later, while still away, I experienced a situation that made my ego get very put out! I was online and read a statement that I felt was in judgment of the Earth Spirit Center for Healing community. My perception was that it was a judgment of something that had occurred in the past, not in the now. I felt the message was not going to be noticed by those it cryptically referred to since those individuals were no longer Facebook contacts with this person, yet the thoughts entering my mind because I had seen it irritated *me*. My ego wanted to spit out counter-questions and go on the defensive. Was this a jab at me, personally? Instead, I took a deep breath (or twenty) and acknowledged the viewpoint and situation in that moment.

I know from my own experience that in challenging times it is very easy to feel overwhelmed, to take things personally, and to allow things to grow large enough due to our egos that we take on the response of suffering.

I like to think heart-to-heart connections are a higher priority than keeping myself out of alignment, so when, four days later, I noted another reference to the community, I took the action of contacting the person to ask if they were okay. Did they want the space to explain more and be fully heard? I for one, was not out to defend or prove anything about the community (at any stage since its opening) or myself. My query on this matter was met with silence, and that is truly okay. My love for the person remains the same to this day.

What I was reminded of through this particular experience is that I wish to have a humorous relationship/connection with my ego (the ego has its purpose and is not "negative"), and that by allowing myself to become open and lighthearted when my ego begins to chatter relentlessly, my time spent feeling hurt, or in suffering, is limited. The Arts of Forgiveness and Unattachment were both part of mastering my emotion in this instance. Forgiveness of myself—because my thoughts were ego based—and Unattachment—because attaching to this person's reality of the community was not my reality. This is not to say the reality was not true for the online commenter, but holding space for this expression and being okay with it, yet remaining true to my own thoughts, was the goal, and what it means to embody peace.

Returning to the awareness gained during my Australia trip, one experience provided the greatest surprise. Prior to the trip, I was anxious about driving the rental car by myself. I'd be on the other side of the road. (Even though I had learned to drive that way when I first had lessons in England, it had been a long time. Could I remember how to navigate roundabouts correctly? What if I were in an accident?) Thus an automatic drive and a GPS unit were musts!

In a nutshell, the rental car experience turned out to be one of inner peace and enjoyment! As I left the airport, the GPS refused to give me directions. I didn't have all day to fight to make it recognize my location, so I gave thanks I had an automatic, took a deep breath and went into intuition mode. The place where I was to stay was under two hours away. I remembered my husband had texted me prior to our parting, "Noosa is north towards the Sunshine Coast, but don't take the Sunshine Coast exit." So I just drove. I even put the radio on and it was such a pleasant drive! Just as I was thinking, *Okay, maybe I need to pull over and ask for directions*, a sign for Noosa Heads appeared! Twenty minutes later, I was on the road leading to my resort. I was in awe! I can't drive to one of my venues in Phoenix to facilitate Chakradance without my GPS, yet there I was in a foreign country, trusting my intuition to be my GPS!

This was a perfect reminder to *take each moment as it comes* and remember that *no moment ever lasts.* These two thoughts can be used as reassurance when we feel concern about a future moment. Life's moments naturally swing like a pendulum. How we respond to these extremes is a choice.

In conclusion, if embodying peace is something you choose to strive for, it is okay. If sometimes, we don't quite respond the way we hope to, that's okay, too. We live, we learn, and we come to see that peace truly is an active process!

Five Minutes: August 16, 2015

Every week, a different member in the community shares a five minute talk with all those present during the Circle of Peace at Earth Spirit Center for Healing. My turn was coming up. I was going to use the time to talk about transparency and vulnerability, but during the week prior, I picked up on signals that directed me towards the subjects of inner peace and mastering our emotions.

Sometimes *Living Peace* and other texts are misinterpreted to mean that one should have an absence of emotion, but I want to highlight that this notion is far from the truth. Embracing or Embodying Peace and mastering emotions is not about suppressing or denying our feelings; rather it entails fully acknowledging and leaning into them.

As a recap for those who have read *Living Peace*, as well as for those who have not, I would like to quote Alaric Hutchinson, *Living Peace*, page 61: *"The reason I work with peace is because it is the foundation that all other uplifting emotions can be built upon. Without peace, all good vibes can easily be washed away when a single external force upsets us and causes us to lose our balance. Without that foundation, our moods are merely leaves blown away by the wind."*

I would like to share a present-day example of why I continue to value peace in my life when it comes to embracing and mastering my emotions.

Last Sunday was my 18th wedding anniversary. A few days prior to this, my husband and I informed our parents and a few close friends that we had started divorce proceedings. We foresaw the shocks that might ripple through our loved ones' minds. We were not prepared to find ourselves the providers of comfort for some of them. Nor did we expect to have to hold the space for them over our decision.

I understand the saying that events like birth, marriage, divorce, illness and death provide an opportunity for us to learn where our genuine relationships are. I heard many varying opinions and judgments regarding our breakup, and I felt them all (especially the implication of words like "failure"). When Ed Sheeran's photograph song came on while I was driving to the lawyer, I cried. My emotions ran like rivers down my face.

When I thought about telling my boys, I felt fear about the end of the year and how it would play out. I even felt doubt at times, questioning whether this truly was best for all. Had I truly tried everything else first to make this work, or not?

So, I sat with all these emotions I began to feel, sometimes with my husband present. We had never heeded outside opinions or questions because we turned over every stone ourselves and felt every emotion first, which was what led us to our life-changing decision.

Mastering our emotions means becoming aware of our true feelings, owning those feelings, listening to the message those feelings are sending us and taking appropriate action. To me, my perception (faulty or healthy) equals surviving or thriving, and I choose to thrive. I recognize that, as people, we love to get attached to what we think we know and to our understanding of the realities we create and/or accept around us. For me, part of embracing peace is stepping back to observe, to witness a situation. As I do so, I am working on non-judgment and implementing compassion for those who have reacted in ways that I did not expect.

When I was younger, I would struggle with not showing my emotions and internalize how I felt, to the point that all this "stuffing" would find not-so-healthy outlets. I would give the "smile and I'm okay" response whenever I was asked; however, this is not what Dunisha Healing™ or *Living Peace* is about. Each of us is responsible for our own emotional wellbeing, but it requires work. We can't remember how we learned to walk as a toddler, but as someone who has witnessed many toddlers in that process, I can tell you that they practice, over and over again, with an attitude to succeed. They fall down, but they get right back up, and this to me is similar to the process of mastering our emotions.

As I work on Inner Peace and keep it at the forefront of my mind each day, I feel that it releases me from both internal and external conflict. I truly do become peace. As the mantra for this tenet denotes, "I am peace."

Tenet Four

Ignorance is Illusion;
We Seek Understanding

By Ignorance, I refer to "not knowing", or "a lack of education".

A simple example: someone cuts you off when you're driving. You might then think they are every impolite name under the sun, but these thoughts are an illusion, not that person truly, because you do not know anything about the "rude" driver but instead make a snap judgment based on one experience. You may have noticed the irony that you don't like it when other people are quick to judge you, but how easy it is for you to make an assessment of another in a split second!

Wednesday, December 2, 2015

Two major themes appeared within my social newsfeed. One was my UK friends' response of disappointment to the UK Parliament's vote to launch air strikes in Syria. The other was American reaction to the mass shooting in California. For the first time in over five years that I'd had a newsfeed with Americans as contacts, I read numerous statuses announcing that my friends were "soon to be new gun owners" because they felt "threatened" and they were "living in very scary times". I sat there and thought about how I felt. I honestly was no more or less scared than when I first set foot in Arizona five years ago.

This made me curious, so I traveled back in my mind to a time prior to my move to the United States. I grew up in a non-gun culture (by which I mean gun ownership is restricted and the laws regarding who may carry one and the reasons for doing so are tightly controlled). I also lived and traveled in other countries with tough gun control laws. I saw and understood how they worked, and I was happy enough to live that way.

Then, prior to the move to the US, my husband received an announcement informing him and his co-workers: "You may not bring handguns into the building. They must be left in the glove compartment of your cars." We were shocked and could not get our heads around this notice—why would anyone want to do *that*? The idea did scare me a little, initially. We joked between ourselves at the time—but it really wasn't so funny—that my husband would now be asking to get shot if someone else at work couldn't handle his opinion. We were flabbergasted!

It wasn't until I moved to Arizona that I began to observe and understand further that this country has a deep and historic attachment to firearms. Unlike Great Britain, which has a Bill of Rights, the USA has a Constitution which includes the Right to Bear Arms. There are approximately 90 guns for every 100 people in the US. More than 85 people a day are killed, and over twice that number are injured with them (*The Guardian*, Gary Younge, 2012).

In the over five years I have lived in Arizona, I have changed my behavior twice to avoid the possibility of a gun incident. Both times, it was a very real concern to me that this might be an outcome, although now they are memories, one of them actually very funny. Had I been armed and trained to use a gun at the time, would it have made a difference in my decision of what to do? No, I believe, fortunately, which is why when Americans state that they feel more secure armed, I don't doubt that. As I said before, I feel no more or less secure than I did on my arrival in the USA, yet some locals around me are now "terrified".

Meeting violence with violence has never achieved much in my mind. However, I must acknowledge a paradox in my thinking. There is a difference between deliberately disengaging to avoid conflict and self defense.

But even though gun ownership is allowed and even encouraged for this purpose in America, I do not expect nor would I ever rely on a member of this country's general public to ever protect me or my children with a gun. I realize the implications are open to interpretation there; but, in observing numerous Americans with heartbreaking firsthand stories of their victimization who still foster peace, empathy, compassion and love—this is the mindset I, too, prefer to foster.

An international example of achievement, hard work and progress is The Northern Ireland Peace Deal, aka the "Good Friday" agreement finally enacted at the end of 1988. This bargain brought an end to thirty years of civil unrest and was unimaginable to many still going through "The Troubles" that year!

"Guns do not kill people; people kill people" is a very popular statement here in America. To me this seems an incomplete statement. I would go further and suggest that **attitudes/beliefs** kill people all over the world. Just as the attitude that they have "the right" to bear arms and to protect themselves runs deep in the American psyche, so, too, does my inner conviction—that our society can function just as well by not embracing guns—run deep.

I reside in a state with a very high rate of children in foster care. Maricopa County alone has 10,000 cases of elder abuse per year. Every 36 minutes a police officer responds to a domestic violence incident in which a child is present. Sex education is not offered in my children's school district. The state ranks 47th in the nation for the quality of education. Many families here earn "too much" but still not enough to pay for their health care. Individuals are in tears because they cannot access needed mental health support and care for loved ones. Boys and girls are thrown out of dogmatic faith communities and made homeless. Many of them are disowned simply because their own interpretation of the religion differs from that of their parents.

You get the picture. I could go on—this state is merely a mirror held up that reflects the entire country—yet rarely does the media espouse a passion for protecting the nation's wellbeing like they do for "gun ownership". There are numerous reasons behind violence. By examining the root causes and taking action, transformation often occurs. There are numerous successful examples within the United States and worldwide. That's where I believe attitude comes in.

Gun control is an emotive topic. My personal feelings about it have moved from not understanding why any society would make guns available to the general public to believing there is no "right" or "wrong" answer particularly, but rather, **what version of society do we prefer?** I am aware that even in asking this question there are many answers. People may use the same descriptive words for their vision of what society should look like, but the ways in which they would achieve their shared vision vary, and that is okay due to compassion and acceptance.

I do believe that gun ownership would not provide me with a sense of security although security is the top reason others cite for ownership. Statistics have proven that having a gun in the house makes living there more dangerous, yet, interestingly, in all the time I have lived here, not one parent has been concerned enough to ask me, when dropping a child off to play, "Is there an unlocked gun in your house?" Of course not, but there could be. For me, parenting in this society involves regular discussions about firearms and what my children are to do or not do if they come into contact with a gun.

This tenet has been invaluable to me in understanding and finding peace regarding America's relationship with weapons. Compassion and Acceptance have become my watchwords. Understanding that "Ignorance" is two-sided. I accept that I am just as "ignorant" of the feelings of others as they are of mine, and I seek to understand. Time in Arizona has exposed me to many opinions and stories as to why some individuals desire guns and have more than one in their home. Many of these accounts are linked to a sense of fear, or to a given right, or to doing the right thing, or even to viewing me as naïve, which doesn't bother me. "Attitude", "Reasonable" and "Responsible"— these are the initial words that come to my mind regarding accessible facts and gun control. No matter how long I reside in the USA, I will continue to make decisions and take actions, however small, to reflect values that I hope will encourage people to connect more deeply instead of further separate.

Another example:

Many years ago, my husband and I had just renewed our vehicle license at a post office in Plymouth, England and were headed back to our car. The license was a paper disc to be displayed on the inside of a vehicle's front windshield and, as we walked, my husband was preparing it for correct display. Suddenly, we heard someone shout, "Hey, you! You there!" We turned around and saw a small car idling, driver at the wheel, as the passenger, a young man, stepped out and continued to yell, "You're deliberately walking slowly to keep us from parking there!"

It was quite a shock so early in the morning. However, we ignored the man and got into the car. But the man kept bellowing at us and then started banging on my husband's window! This triggered me to get out of the car. I told him, "Excuse me, we have no plans to hold you up, so please, leave our car alone!"

This only fueled him to argue further. I could see the police station from where we were since the car was parked on the top level of a multi-storey garage. I tried to make a call, but there was no carrier signal on my phone. The man continued with his aggressive speech, and I felt threatened. It was at this point I noticed that other people were watching us but keeping their distance.

The person the man was with sat very quietly in the car. Then it dawned on me, the driver's friend clearly had something going on to behave this way. I also accepted that arguing with him wasn't going to make him see my viewpoint. He was unable to understand anything but how he felt, so shifting my approach brought me some calm. I looked at him and began to see him differently. I knew we had to get out of this situation as quickly and calmly as possible, so I lowered my voice and my defenses. Maybe he was drunk. Maybe he had had a rough 24 hours that I knew nothing about. Maybe he had mental health challenges. I had no idea what was truly behind his anger, but in that moment I felt compassion for him, and I began to agree with him.

He was thrown off balance by this. Though he cursed and expressed, "If you ever have children, I hope they're ugly!" he began to wind his rant down. The driver now felt he could get out and guide his passenger back to their car. This encounter, I believe, really helped me to further free myself from judgment when dealing with someone who seems overly angry or irritated.

I actively work at employing the skills of compassion. It may not always be easy, but it means I am prepared to give up the need to be right or justified and instead be more present in the moment. I view it as an opportunity to learn more about others and myself.

Since I began using social media—without searching for these responses—I have received numerous apologies from individuals I went to school with who bullied me at some point. It expanded my mind and heart to learn that one boy had been physically abused by a parent during our primary and elementary school years, and that was why he turned it around on me. People in pain do inflict pain on others.

I have found this tenet most useful in situations with individuals who are highly emotive whether online or in person. Compassion alongside Pause, Process and Respond (PPR) assist me in keeping my responses in check. Acceptance also goes a long way. I have found that two side effects of learning this tenet are: needing to express my opinions less, and having no hard opinions, since I am aware that I often do not have the full picture. Now, I rarely volunteer my opinions unless they are specifically asked for or I've taken time to think carefully about the intention of my words.

Tenet Five

Chaos is Illusion;
We seek Harmony

This tenet takes me back to a memory of a few years ago, when a man came to the front door and I overheard this conversation he had with my husband:

Man: "Isn't the world a much worse place than it used to be, with all the wars, famine, high unemployment, sickness and plagues? This is what the Bible said would happen near the end of time. Doesn't this concern you?"

Husband: "No, I can't say I agree with your view."

Man: "You don't see these things happening?"

Husband: "I do, but with today's technology, information can be shared faster and travels further, which allows us to know more about what's happening than we did in the past. Besides, the media often focuses only on the most fearsome stories, so no, I don't believe the world is worse off."

The conversation went back and forth. Tthe man became more and more frustrated because my husband would not change his stance and agree that all the chaos was something to get anxious and fearful over. When my husband concluded with, "Well, I feel happy," the man grudgingly went on his way.

Two men with two different perspectives: this is what chaos is, differing perspectives. One man was attached to the idea of global chaos, resisting, holding on, panic-based, while the other was unknowingly using this tenet's Arts of Allowing and Objectivity segments to remain calm, serene, and "happy".

I believe this ties in well with Alaric Hutchinson's passage (p78, *Living Peace*), *"One of the major causes of the perpetuation of chaos is the idea of chaos itself. We attach ourselves to the judgments we make in the chaotic present moment, forgetting that life is ever in motion, and that the darkness tonight will be met with the light in the morning. Every hurricane eventually subsides, every volcano settles, and every raging forest fire gives way to new life. The true reality is that balance is always present and can be found in life if we desire to look for it. It is our job as the living embodiment of peace to always look beyond the surface level of chaos to find the harmony within."*

This is a tenet that can be wide open to misinterpretation, one in which some people may believe a person is in denial for not seeing "reality" or for not agreeing with their perception of chaos. So it is within this dialogue about this tenet that I want to stress that, working as I am on embodying peace, this is not my perception.

I find that by focusing my attention on resistance— especially when I cannot do anything about the situation—I am only going to make myself anxious, frustrated, or angry. However, by focusing on my inner peace, I am becoming more harmonious, allowing myself a healthier approach should I then find myself in a situation in which I can have a say or exert some influence.

A good example is the education system. Here in Arizona the system is very different from those I was brought up in. I have heard many opinions about the state's education system, opinions that vary widely in perception (and that includes perceptions of chaos!). As a non-US citizen, the vote is understandably not available to me, but I do have a choice about how I seek harmony. I can choose to sit around and verbally-castigate the system, or I can homeschool my children or I can even choose to move country. The path I have taken is to focus more closely on my children's progress, see the bigger picture (including how they are doing socially and emotionally), and volunteer both in and out of the classroom. I love engaging with a roomful of children, each shining in their own way. By doing these things, I believe I have chosen harmony instead of chaos in this instance.

Another personal example I wanted to share regarding the tenet, Chaos is an Illusion; We seek Harmony, is my experience of an American election. This is the fourth country in which I have observed election habits and the first time I actually found myself crying in private at what I've witnessed. It took time for me to realize that I was attached to judgments, particularly other peoples' judgments of one another. I observed that if an individual chooses to vote a particular party, it can mean (to the person casting judgment) that they are "Un-American". From this, a plethora of unnecessary insults ensues. Observing this, I resisted; I could not accept it, to the point it wore me down. No kidding, I was actually exhausting myself with my resistance. Interesting really, when I was absolutely fine about not having a vote, yet I was, nonetheless, absorbing all of the low-vibe gunk the candidates and society at large were slinging!

In 2011, what triggered these private tears was seeing some of my American friends with raised stress and anxiety levels—particularly over their much-needed and unaffordable health care treatments—or for other friends on social media who were overly irritated by people who held differing perspectives from theirs. Most of us want to see those we care about happy! I felt then that everywhere I looked there was a density of people who expressed that they felt overwhelmed and helpless. I had never before experienced such an intensity of scared and angry emotions.

At the present time, the 2016 presidential campaign is underway, and I value how much I have grown on a personal level when I compare my reactions then to those I have now. On reflection, I can see that earlier, I had wanted so desperately for things to be different in my environment. I was struggling, wishing more of the people of this country could react differently, and while I still don't condone some of the opinions or actions I hear or see, I have become aware of allowing, more active in managing the experience (for one, I've reduced the time I spend online to minimize the stress it engenders in me), and I'm being more objective and letting go, so the level of peace I now experience within is considerably raised.

In *The Power of Now,* Chapter 9, "Beyond Happiness & Unhappiness there is Peace" (p.148), Eckhart Tolle has a wonderful passage that describes what I've learned perfectly:

> *When something dreadful happens to me or someone close to me—accident, illness, pain of some kind, or death—I can pretend that it isn't bad, but the fact remains that it is bad, so why deny it?*

> *You are not pretending anything. You are allowing it to be as it is, that's all. This "allowing to be" takes you beyond the mind with the resistance patterns that create the positive-negative polarities.*

Tenet Six

Duality is Illusion;
We seek Transcendence

Duality is concerned with many opposites, for example: light, dark; good, evil; positive, negative; health and sickness, etc. Material items and experiences just exist, but humans label them and define them. The way in which we interpret our environments can cause suffering and stagnancy, or it can lead to an outcome that facilitates joy and forward motion in our self-development.

I was raised within predominantly Catholic environments in England. I consider myself fortunate that I do not recall the word "evil" being focused upon in the same way I have observed it to be in America.

"Evil" is not a word generally found in my vocabulary. This can be traced to having read *The Man who Mistook his Wife for a Hat* by Oliver Sacks. The book examines cases of brain function. The insight I gained by reading about these abnormalities—that the brain truly is a precious organ and that it's all too easy for society to take brain function for granted—made a huge impression on me as a teenager. Sacks' writing concerning his cases embodied compassion and this influenced me greatly to not refer to others as "evil". I have felt that—even though I observe society desiring a world filled with peace, love and harmony—they continue to use the word "evil", which is alienating and blocks the flow that would create such peace, love and harmony.

Research scans have proven that low activity in specific areas of the frontal and temporal lobes link to self-control and empathy. Of course, there are always variations. Even with the same scan results, not everyone will behave in the same manner. Oliver Sacks' work has always driven me to seek the bigger picture. I am aware it is not a popular mindset to have, but I believe I personally am encouraged to consider more than what is immediately apparent.

My understanding is that collectively, people in society feel a need to understand the why of everything, yet this is something that simply cannot be done. The collective consciousness of a society or group finger points and desires someone, often anyone but themselves, to be held responsible for "evil". Nations like the UK and America are known (as collective groups) for not tolerating child abuse, especially when the victim is very young. However, it is like a switch is thrown when the same individual reaches an age when their actions no longer seem cute and innocent. Then our current society has a blunt "grow up and deal with it" attitude toward the older child or adult who has experienced (given or received) trauma. Compassion for either the victim or the perpetrator often goes out the window, and revenge is sought instead.

Consider the case of Cecil Clayton. Cecil was a Missouri man who was missing a part of his brain (his scan showed a literal hole in his head due to a sawmill accident). He had an IQ of 71 with no violent history prior to this accident or the crime he committed—murdering a Sheriff's Deputy after a domestic disturbance. Yet, he was still executed in March, 2015—even though he had a medical condition that caused his lack of control. The uncontrollable act was "evil" and thus had to be done away with.

Differences of thought regarding revenge or blame and what is "right" or "wrong" have always existed. For me the question is: Which thought is of a higher nature and productive, since the effects of revenge have been shown not to make us feel better?

An experiment, devised by Kevin Carlsmith and his colleagues, set up a group investment game. The subjects were students who formed separate groups. If everyone in a group cooperated, members of that group would benefit equally from the game. If an individual refused to invest their money, that individual would benefit unreasonably at the group's expense.

One person in each group was aware of the experiment and was given the task of convincing everyone to invest the same dollar amount. When it was time to hand over the money, the person who'd been "planted" defected, thus earning more than the other players. Most players reacted with anger. Therefore, when some groups were given an opportunity to spend their own earnings from the game to financially punish the group's defector, they gladly took it!

A survey was then taken to measure feelings after the experiment. Groups who were allowed to seek punishment reported feeling considerably worse than groups who were not given this opportunity. Groups who had opted to seek punishment said they thought they would have felt worse had they not been given that occasion for revenge, and not the other way around. The groups unable to seek revenge said they thought they would have felt better if they had the chance to punish the individual, even though they were the ones who did, in fact, feel better. In a nutshell, both groups thought revenge would feel good, but their documented feelings showed differently (Kevin Carlsmith, May 2008, Journal of Personality and Social Psychology, Vol.95. No.6).

A compassionate response often attracts criticism that the individual is "too soft" or inaccurately "doesn't believe in holding someone accountable". I view it as natural to feel anger, but focusing on "evil" often elicits thoughts, impulses and emotions that are of the same conscious-ness as those one claims to abhor.

I have often heard or read the statement, "A rapist should experience rape in prison." This makes no sense to me since violence met with violence simply maintains and keeps the cycle of abuse going.

I choose to work hard to transcend my thoughts when dealing with those who feel this way and also when faced with contradictory situations. For instance, over the past two years, the state of Arizona has failed to submit proof of compliance or assurances that it has been meeting federal prison rape laws. The Prison Rape Elimination Act (PREA) passed in 2003 was created with the intention to "provide for the analysis of the incidence and effects of prison rape in Federal, State, and local institutions to provide information, resources, recommendations and funding to protect individuals from prison rape" (Prison Rape Elimination Act, 2003). This act sets many standards, including how to strip search opposite gender and transgender prisoners.

The state lost out on $200,000 in federal funding for non-compliance. So yes, I have to work to transcend my thoughts concerning this situation; otherwise, they may become similar in dualistic nature to those of the persons who believe rapists should be raped. This is especially critical if I am not prepared to take action on a deeper level to seek change within the prison system to assure the laws are upheld. Persistence of dualistic thought can feed on itself and make an individual suffer more, mentally and physically, due to the conflict and stress within the mind that then causes dis-ease in the body.

When society labels people as "evil" or "monsters", it doesn't take too long for it to become acceptable to treat them poorly. We are taught that revenge is strong and compassion is weak. We are taught that flexing our powers to achieve what we perceive as justice is more important than love, even though the heart of most of humanity's spiritual beliefs is the teaching of said "love".

In September, 2005, I began writing to American prisoners. I now write to six prisoners regularly. Whenever I can, I honor the card requests I receive through the prison pal community. Initially, I wrote because I had experienced the joy of writing to and receiving letters from my granny as a girl. The prisoner correspondence started as an "I can do that; I love writing and receiving letters" thing, and has turned into far more.

These correspondences have shone a light on that bigger picture I referred to earlier. Whether it comes down to genetics, environment or a combination of the two, I have observed that separation only breeds more separation. No matter what their history or emotional state is, prisoners are human beings who deserve space to be held for them the same as any other person.

I have witnessed that some of these men were touched deeply by the unconditional love of women who wrote them. Prison pen pal correspondences can be immensely inspirational for those involved. Learning about each other tends to naturally occur. Such correspondences can nurture the growth of individuals on the "inside" as well as on the "outside", and encourage them to take more positive actions in their lives. I have been introduced to persons who showed up initially as their authentic selves, with no agenda other than to be a friendly support in their "pals" environment who later became life partners of the prisoners they wrote. Accepting someone where that person is now, not where they were in their past, is a quality worth appreciating.

One particular pal I wrote to began sending me evidence of the educational classes he had attended and passed. This was a sign of his growing sense of self. Healthy self-esteem and sense of pride are not always developed in every childhood. (Have you noticed that people with pleasant attitudes of self esteem tend to treat others from a place of kindness and respect?)

I will never forget one letter in which this man shared proudly that he gave some soap to a man of a different race who was struggling with a disability. He declared he would never have dreamed of doing that in the past, and it shocked the other man, too, but he gave the soap because he felt it was the better choice to make. This may seem an insignificant act, but it was an incredible moment in this man's formerly selfish and racist life, one that I recognized and acknowledged him for.

The same man told me he had never had a real friend before, "so thank you for being a friend." All I was doing was writing and receiving letters, nothing I consider extraordinary! (But he did.) With his background—he was raised in a gang and became Top Dog of that gang—what were his odds of turning 18 and suddenly conforming to societal expectations to be a "good citizen" when he had no prior experience of what healthy love and support or concept of what being a "good citizen" meant? He shared freely with me that I had given him an opportunity to experience something radically different from what he was used to.

I know another man on death row who is one of the most genuine, positive, grateful, down-to-earth, reasonable individuals I have ever met in my lifetime. Despite his life story and the place where he now resides, he has created a solid sense of family for himself through his pen pals. He did not have this support prior to his arrest, and we remain hopeful that his case be viewed and factually corrected to allow his release.

Sincerely, each of these individuals has taught me so much about humankind that it is hard to put into words how grateful I am to them.

Had I held a dualistic mindset, I probably would never have started writing to those on the "inside", or my judgment of them might have hindered my learning. Instead my perception unlocked the doors to my compassion and led me up the steps of transcendence.

"Unconditional LOVE is the outward expression of inner peace" ~ Alaric Hutchinson

I feel it is important to recognize when we start to transcend duality and check in with our perceptions, and to note when we are practicing the Art of Unity by focusing on our inner peace. I feel that this is when our level of consciousness rises, which then leads to greater, more focused action. This motion then creates from a place of peace and inspiration, which in turn directs unifying change and harmony in our world.

Tenet Seven

Release the Mundane

Mundane refers to the very ordinary, common, earthly matters rather than the spiritual. It is very easy for people to focus on issues that use up energy in a tiresome way. For example, a couple arguing over housework. Perhaps one of them dislikes that they are the one always doing certain chores and the other feels that they should not have to take over these same chores for various reasons (such as their long work hours). Of course, it is of value that this issue is resolved, but on a consciousness level this is mundane. When they take a step back from the argument, the couple starts to focus on what they consider the more important things in life to be, and they are then able to see the larger picture and realize the insignificance of their disagreement.

An awareness of my thoughts and what they lead me to feel is a great indicator of what Layer of Consciousness I am sitting in (referencing the 5 Layers of Consciousness explored in *Living Peace*, the mundane being the outer, lowermost level). A fantastic instance of this concerns a situation that arose one day while I was on social media, and a friend I admire—who is also an author, international traveler and visionary—mentioned that she was feeling a moment of isolation.

For whatever reason, my brain flooded with thoughts about this statement, so much so that I just *had* to share them. This would have been fine, except for a few things. One, I had 2% battery power left on my phone; two, I had to be somewhere and was pushing it on time; three, I needed to use the bathroom, too! But, I made sending my thoughts to my friend a priority. As I was typing, my brain was overwhelmed with responses, most I did not include in my hurry. I let her know that, though I was in a rush, I hoped her spirit would soon be uplifted. I said I had enjoyed a talk she had recently posted. I added that "isolation is an illusion", although acknowledging any feeling is always beneficial. I also included a link to a short, past video of Alaric's about Joy and Conscious

Expansion without knowing *why* I had chosen that particular one. (You can probably tell where this is headed!)

Before long, I received an appreciative response; however, all my mind could focus on was this portion of the reply: *"Didn't you see my post about dropping 'it's an illusion' when someone expresses how they feel? LOL. I know it is well-meaning but it makes people feel as though they are not heard. That how they feel is just brushed away."*

On reading this, my heart tore in horror and grief. In no way did I mean to imply this person's (or anyone's) feelings should be brushed away! To be honest, I was also exceptionally embarrassed. How was I supposed to speak fluently on the subject of peace and creating it within, when I had just done what I did? I thought, *I suck at this! Why did I not put my brakes on and wait to share until I had the time to express my thoughts more fully and not in such an "itty bitty" manner? Why am I so damn sensitive? I really haven't moved anywhere in my practice; I am still way too sensitive to the words of others. Even this person is far more proficient at and advanced in awareness than I am. Why did I even go there with my sharing?*

Before I responded, I took another look at the link I had sent. It wasn't very relevant, but it did mention "butterfly", a keyword that applied to this person's life, so the video didn't seem totally redundant, after all.

As I re-watched the video, my mind slowly unwound and relaxed. Gradually, I became aware that my reaction over this interaction with my friend was obsessive, and then I perceived that my obsession over this interaction was mundane, from ego and unnecessary. So, I sent her another message to say that I honestly did not mean to imply that her (or anyone's) feelings should be brushed away! I admitted that I could've put my brakes on before sending her the initial message, and I thanked her for being her, especially since her response triggered inspiration in me. (I didn't say that the inspiration came in the form of reflecting on this tenet, but that was what happened.)

The reply of, "All is good and okay", made me laugh, because it truly was; my loving intention had not been missed; I had only been causing myself suffering, so this was a great lesson!

Working with Gratitude and Trust helps me release the mundane. I have gone more deeply into Gratitude lately, but in this instance, I fell back on Trust, acknowledging that many of my thoughts about the mistake I made in this example stemmed from placing too many "shoulds", and other high expectations, on myself. To feel at my best, I did not need to get back on the hamster wheel of previous thought patterns. I needed to trust the process and where I was at in that moment as part of it.

By releasing the mundane, which is part of the Whole, this recognition and discharge can be turned into a spiritual practice to assist us in reaching Unity.

Another instance: With today's avenues, such as Facebook, in which to share news, my soon to be ex-husband and I chose to avoid jumping into the social media arena until we were further along in the divorce proceedings. Even then, we were very specific about sharing only with those we felt needed to know. The reason for this was our concern over how people might respond. Sure enough, when we finally posted the news that we were going our separate ways, we found that our gut instincts were correct. We were then met primarily with people's projections, assumptions and judgments. We also chose not to disclose our reasons, which irritated and understandably puzzled some. We accepted that people were going to have their own theories and that we did not need to fuel or challenge any of them. Our priority was to ourselves and our two young sons.

If I had chosen to make the words and projections of others a priority, the process would have been far more stressful. At one point, I was disappointed that some folks I considered to be my long-term, good friends had reacted as they had. One friend even laughed when told. That was it, laughter and a beaming smile. I felt shocked and wondered whether this person had heard me correctly before I paused, processed and realized that I was holding my friend to my expectations of how *I* would respond to the news of a friend's divorce, and that was unfair. It did, however, give me an indication of whom I could trust on a deeper level friendship-wise.

The tools that helped me release the mundane (attachment to the physical world) in this case were: the Art of Gratitude and the Art of Trust. I remembered to have Gratitude for all the small things in life (even the "manure"). Gratitude leads to joy, so I could not be grumpy and in a state of joy at the same time! The Art of Trust was also important because some people around me had fears that I could have allowed to affect me otherwise. I understood the root of these fears stemmed from concern for me, but they could not hide their anxiety and made comments that unleashed a need in me to be the one to hold space for them. After dealing with this, I returned to Gratitude for all those who *could* hold space for me in a supportive, non judgmental way.

Overall, even though I am now on my own, I am not scared to "be alone" as I view this as an illusion I create for myself. I have come to feel deeply this quote from Julian of Norwich that we often recite at the Center, "All shall be well, and all shall be well, and all manner of thing shall be well."

I also receive Trust and inspiration from others. Some I know on a personal level, others I have never met, and their paths, though different, hold a light up that illuminates and excites me. Witnessing the ways in which they change their challenges into opportunities reminds me that I, too, can create my own strength and inner Trust that does not rely on ego but is instead Spirit-led Guidance. However, I can only do this by paying attention to the basic, mundane bricks of my thoughts, impulses, and emotions. I believe Gratitude is the key to rising above this layer, so much so, that I have written on this subject alone in the chapter which follows.

The Value of GRATITUDE

Dear Parent,

I couldn't help but overhear your comments about your child being too slow in their swim event; in fact I heard you grumbling not once, but four times. Maybe you are having an off day. I hope it improves.

I looked at those eight lanes of children in the present moment and said to myself, "How grateful I am that those children can enjoy functioning limbs." But it gets better than that! I also thought, "I am grateful that all eight can swim to any degree (after all, swimming is a valuable skill and can be fun, too)."

I am grateful that these children have an adult with the means to put fuel in their car to allow them to escort the kids to this meet. I am grateful so many of us here appear to value exercise for our children and on such a beautiful day, too. One that's not too hot or cold for Arizona.

I wonder if you are aware that 16 volunteers stepped up to time the children's events. One volunteer less would have meant you or I would have had to volunteer, assuming we didn't want a cancelled meet. Thank you volunteers!

Notice there are only two swim schools participating today. I am grateful that this will only be a two-hour, not a four-hour plus event. What a nice surprise!

Did you get that the programs were <u>only</u> $2—and not a dollar more? Yes, I heard you commenting about the price, too. Now, I am feeling gratitude for the time someone took to put those programs together and for the ink and paper contributed.

Now I see you fiddling on your phone, as many parents are, provided with a distraction when their child isn't swimming. First world luxury, being utilized with so little gratitude. I hear some people feel naked without their phone on them these days. Wonder how they'd feel to have to actually go naked as some in the third world still must. I gaze above me at all the airplanes, a constant flow of them ascending or descending to a safe landing... If that's not something spectacular to be grateful for... pretty amazing!

Then my attention is turned to the clean drinking water that many of us are sipping. Watching as my other son trots off to use a reasonably clean, readily available bathroom because he's been drinking so much of this good water—I am so, so grateful!

Before I know it, Dear Parent, I've gone from sensing gratitude for you, to gratitude for what is in my reality, to gratitude for both realities and even what appears as contrast in them at this time. How amazingly happy and joyous I feel right in this moment! I feel so grateful to watch our children partake in such a wonderful sport performance and that all of us are breathing!

The practice of gratitude is found in Alaric Hutchinson's *Living Peace* in the meditation section. A tool to use with the practice of gratitude is the Art of Belief (*Living Peace*, Mastery of Thought, page 9). As in my example of the swim parent with the belief that their child was too slow—though I initially felt inclined to roll my eyes—I adjusted my thoughts and beliefs so as to feel much better about that situation and was reminded that it really didn't matter what place a child came in, as long as they had fun. I was also aware that focusing on that present moment and that fun were what mattered most in the grand picture.

Now, I know that most of us here are aware of the good in our lives and practice being grateful, but I also understand that this practice comes much easier when things are going well, or we feel we're in a good place. Sometimes (using my own experience),-my heart may not quite agree with the logic of my head and I get a bit stuck, even though—logically—I know being thankful will help shift my emotions. So, what else helps—toolbox-wise— with getting unstuck when I am experiencing my inner "Grumpy"?

If you are like me, and you also have an inner Grumpy, a daily gratitude journal, whether in the form of written words, photos, or drawings (or any combination thereof) is of great benefit. It takes time for a new habit to form, and the daily action of keeping such a journal sets the attitude of gratitude in motion.

It's also helpful, when you're really stuck with Grumpy, to simply acknowledge that you are human and start small. It may be easier just to listen to a favorite music track or break the practice down even further. Toilet rolls, for example, are some of my preferred items to focus gratitude on—small yet significant—what would we do without them?

Gratitude, in the purest form within my understanding, means there is no comparison to others. Being thankful is about seeking appreciation for our own reality in the Now, no matter the situation. When we find gratitude, really feel it, we rise to joy. Joy overflows and becomes a healthy way to experience ourselves and others.

Research has shown that those who consistently practice gratitude reap many benefits, benefits that extend to our physical health, emotional and social wellbeing, work prospects and personality zones. It is a practice worth exercising whenever we can.

Gratitude can be transformational. Its impact is not to be underestimated when we are in survival mode. I invite you today to find (or re-examine) the-smallest seed of gratitude within you, experience it as deeply as you can and let that feeling flood every cell of your body.

Finally, I would like to share a quote:

"Gratitude unlocks the fullness of life. It turns what we have into enough, and more. It turns denial into acceptance, chaos to order, confusion to clarity. It can turn a meal into a feast, a house into a home, a stranger into a friend.

Gratitude makes sense of our past, brings peace for today and creates a vision for tomorrow." ~ Melody Beattie

Tenet Eight

Release Knowing

There is a paradox to this tenet, for in releasing attachments to what we know, we also release our attachments to what we don't know! When we attach to *I know* this becomes a hinderance to learning and also limits our actions. I have lost count of the times in the past I have attached *I know* to the way I think someone will react to some news I have to share. "*I know* they won't be happy" or "*I know* they won't support me" or "*I know* this idea will be met with rejection." Did you notice the pattern of knowing and negatives? Perhaps you have done this, too?

I would like to suggest putting all your "I knows" down and allowing surprise in! Even if the reaction does go the way of your gut feeling, this is okay, but opportunities to have new, positive experiences in life can be missed when we believe we *know* what will happen. For instance, the first time I agreed to partake in karaoke was while accompanying a friend to sing in Arizona. I pushed myself to get past the "this will sound terrible" thought process, allowed myself to have some courage and vulnerability and proceeded to sing three songs. The experience was not as horrific as I had imagined it would be. People cheered, and one stranger came up to congratulate me when I sang a song by his favorite English rock band. The experience set me up for partaking in future karaoke sessions.

What we think we *know* about a situation is only one perspective, a limited view, not the full picture.

I must admit, it took me awhile to give my attention to writing about this tenet, which I find interesting. Ask any Dunisha student, and they will freely mention the tenet they find harder to work on than any other. For me, it's this one.

Around the age of seven or so, I had a recurring dream each night for a period of time. It involved child labor in a prison, and the guards in the dream were physically and sexually abusive. During this time, I did not want to wear nightdresses and preferred pajamas because the dream seemed less severe if I wore p.j.'s. As I grew older and recalled this dream, I couldn't figure out how I knew about sexual abuse at such a young age, even being mindful of the fact that our brains have been proven to distort memories during recall and the same would apply to childhood dreams. The very few people I was comfortable confiding in shared the same thought that had occurred to me—perhaps I had been abused at some point outside my family unit and had suppressed it very deeply. Another suggestion was that via my dreams I was remembering a past life.

Throughout my life since then, I've wondered whether I should make an effort to find out more about those dreams. Not long after I became a member at Earth Spirit Center for Healing, I started to dream very vividly with practically everyone I had met in AZ showing up in them over time! The dreams seemed to be full of "messages" and were very inspiring, so again I thought, "Perhaps I need to *know* about this particular childhood dream."

During my Dunisha training, I sat with myself and asked myself honestly why I needed to *know*. An Emotional Freedom Technique (EFT) session had already provided an answer for me, but part of me still desired an actual memory to confirm what I felt but did not clearly remember. It took vulnerability to be honest with myself in all that I felt or didn't feel when I questioned myself about this. The answer I got from myself was that this was an issue that needed no further clarification. Not knowing the absolute was okay in this instance.

In contemplating this chapter, I also wondered what first impression I had given people over the years. I was curious to see if there were any first impressions that had accurately gauged a previous emotional state—distant, stressed, depressed. I asked my friends via social media for three words to describe their first impressions of me. As the responses began to come in, I saw a fascinating correlation—during the times I experienced high emotions, the people who had met me then described me with words like "tall, fun, accent". When my emotions were subdued, those who met me then called me "smiling, quiet, British". When I was showing up authentically in life, the qualities they described went below surface level (e.g. "wholesome, giver, compassionate" or "loyal, kind, action-oriented") even if they had only known me a short time or had never met me in person.

This little exercise also gave rise to the thought that perhaps we see others from the perspective of how we feel about ourselves. There were a couple of "shy, unsure, nervous" responses. When I recalled meeting these respondents, I was not entirely content with the environment we met in, and thus my stress was reflected. Perhaps, they, in turn, saw me, to a degree, in light of the emotions *they* might have felt. In saying this, I release from judging and merely observe.

Preparing for the role of the Dunisha Master has been my paradox. At times, I have felt that I do not *know* enough, yet when I am centered, I can see I have learned, observed and practiced, and I can trust in this to assist me to perceive with Unattachment, to let go of what I think I *know.*

Tenet Nine

Release Self

To be honest, when I initially heard the tenet, "Release Self" I thought, "Hmm..." but then realized this was the perfect opportunity to share, because releasing self involves the ego, and I find the ego fascinating. When balance occurs in our lives, our egos are neither too large (over-confident) nor do they devalue who we are (low self esteem). It is important to realize that before one can release the self, one needs a self to release.

The idea of releasing the self can cause confusion. What does that mean exactly? Release of self is about releasing attachments we have about ourselves that cause situations of contrast in our lives. It does not mean that we place our needs and dreams behind another's.

In the past, I thought I was clear on my sense of self, but at the core, my sense of self worth actually fluctuated quite a bit. As a mother, it was very easy to forget who I was. Mothers give (and are encouraged to give) a lot to their children; often feeling like they must be an emotional anchor due to societal expectations to keep peace or provide the harmony in a family, and at the same time, put the needs of all family members before their own.

When I was 18, I trained in childcare and learned to work with the parents. Having never been a parent myself, I was always very careful to be understanding and supportive of my clients; nonetheless, when my first son came along, my understanding deepened considerably. My labor at the maternity unit was very peaceful in one respect. The midwives asked if they could leave me and my husband alone with the call beeper so that they could assist another lady who was screaming in pain in the room next door. I had two looping music tracks playing on the portable stereo. With my husband's hand to dig my nails into, and visualizing the pain walking out of the room with each contraction, I was in a fairly good mindset to let them attend to this lady. That was until later in the day, during the pushing stage of labor when the midwives announced they were going to call the doctor on duty in to see me due to their concerns over the progression of my labor. The doctor decided it was an emergency situation and demanded, "Stop pushing before you brain damage the baby."

What came after my son's birth was challenging, to say the least. I questioned my worth as a mother because, initially, all I could focus on was what I wasn't doing or feeling. Not long after his arrival, we were moved to the Intensive Care Unit for newborns. Due to extreme jaundice, he narrowly missed having to have a complete blood transfusion. The trauma of all this, plus the emergency caesarean, caused me to feel a fatigue that was so deep, I can only describe it as feeling like a zombie! The UK government was then running a campaign with the slogan "Breast is Best". I also felt like I was a failure for feeding him via breast for just ten days before switching over to formula milk. That feeling of failure only intensified when I went out and bought him a pacifier, shoving it in his mouth so I could cope with his only means of communication, crying!

I became lost and isolated. I had attachments (to the idea of what a good mum was) and I was in ego, in duality, because I was stuck in high judgment of myself. I had this idea that new mothers were supposed to enjoy their newborns—other first time mothers looked so happy and beautiful, beaming with high energy—and there I was, so extremely dog tired that at times, my husband—who worked two hours' drive away and also required his sleep to leave early in the morning—would nudge me awake because I would not hear our son cry even though he was in the same room in his Moses basket! At one point, I remember reading a library book that suggested that if a parent with post-partum depression could manage to spend twenty minutes of quality time a day with their baby before they reached their first birthday, it would be good enough for their development in the long run. I made it my daily goal to reach that minimum or extend it. Throw in all those fun postpartum hormones, and it was certainly an interesting time.

This is a tenet I am still working on, and those in the Dunisha Sanctuary gently call me out whenever I begin to wrap myself in my "bad mum" illusions. I have moments of strongly questioning how I handle motherhood, especially now that my eldest son has almost hit his teenage years!

In working with release of self, we learn to look at a situation without judgment. It means relinquishing those judgments— a.k.a. attachments—and viewing humanity as a whole rather than as separate pieces. Without judgment, I aim to foster unconditional love. I now lack the desire to nitpick on others about how they live their lives, yet I have observed that in America, the media and politicians alike feed to us what and who we are as a society, and some of those notions about "American greatness" are unfounded, simply an opinion without evidential roots. Statistics on the overcrowded prison population in this country alone offer the insight that this country is not necessarily the best or safest place in the world to live, and that many live in isolation.

Alaric expresses in his book that humans have the habit of identifying with past experiences, and I have come to see that the times I have activated that habit of harking to the past have been limiting.

After a few years at my first nanny job, I managed to go to university as a mature student. I had a dual major in Sociology/ Psychology. Mathematics had always been a challenge, yet I was allowed to start this course of study even though I had received an E, not a C, in my 16-year-old exams for completion of my General Certificates of Secondary Education (GCSES).

In the educational system of England, grades are given by letters, A being the highest mark, C being minimum standard expected in the core subjects of English, Mathematics and Science to generally move on to further study or get a job, then dropping each letter alphabetically by a percent through F meaning the student has failed the exam. Thus, that E meant I hovered just above the brink of failure, barely passing the GCSES, so getting into university was something for which I was highly grateful.

Research Methods in Psychology was interesting. The low ego part of me was fearful and wondered how on earth would I pass, but the first year was okay. The second year and part of my third and final year—oh, boy!—but somehow I did it. I studied both alone and with the help of my Psychology friends to get to the point that my mathematics in the research skills understanding went beyond that of my degreed engineer husband. Though I have since forgotten that information, and I would be in no hurry to repeat the experience, I passed and gained my Diploma of Higher Education (DipHE) despite the low self-esteem I secretly harbored and the attachment I'd had to being mathematically challenged.

At some point on the journey of life, a person may or may not become aware that it is possible to observe a flower without labeling and confining it as such. Whether this understanding is reached or not is neither "right" nor "wrong". One becomes aware through personal, self-development. The experience of hitting rock bottom may lead to an awakening of personal expansion, but the moment someone labels a flower a flower, it ceases to be anything else, a limitation has been placed upon it.

This is best demonstrated in terms of labeling others. The spoken or unspoken labeling of others may appear to be a good tool for organization and helping to make sense of the world, yet that label comes from a place of ego. It is ego perception that feeds the illusion of others as "separate" or "similar". The ego enjoys comparing and focusing on lack; this in turn creates suffering and limitation.

When we no longer identify with the ego, we don't give it fuel. This does not mean squashing the ego but integrating it. The ego can often be a beautiful learning obstacle for all at some point.

Why do we release ego? We release it to allow for expansion of ourselves and others, to grow, whether that growth takes the form of releasing a victim mentality or becoming more honestly humble. We do this by releasing self through the arts of relinquishment and love. This provides freedom and the joyous ability to see ourselves and others via a sense of peace. We are all much more than we can ever imagine.

Very few people believe me when I say I have no expectations to become a grandparent, or that my sons should marry anyone, or have children, or go to a university, or even outlive me. It is not my business to dream the details of their journey, though I do hope they travel their paths with kindness, joy and a healthy self esteem. The moment I label them, I limit them. So, if I must place limits (I recognize it happens regardless of my intent because our society works with labels) I hope the labels I resort to are of a kinder nature. Labels can literally kill if a society chooses them to, as with those labeled as Jews in WWII. We are always more than boxes with labels on them!

By being in the present moment, by choosing thoughts that are of a higher nature, I continue to practice! We are not our pasts, we are the present, and we are much more than our ego-perceived selves.

Everything is Impermanent;
Change is the only Constant

This came to me as an area to delve into on Sunday, February 15, 2015, mainly because of the switch in facilitation roles in our community at Earth Spirit Center for Healing.

If I had been told, the very first time I entered Earth Spirit Center, that I would sit on the speaker's cushion, holding the space at the front for an hour all by myself, I would have laughed, said "No way!", and continued with my quiet life. Had I been told, in 2014, "You are going to sit on that cushion", I would have been mortified. Then, as the time approached, I would have sucked up my emotions but still desperately hoped that people would opt to sleep in or find better things to do. I believed (with the sense of awkwardness I carried within me back then) that if it happened, it would only be because the person they really wanted to see and hear would not be there.

Yet, when I was asked to sit on the cushion on the 15th of February, I found myself breaking into a smile. Even though I initially got the "UH-OH!" feeling, I managed to flip it right around and view the invitation as an opportunity. I was over the moon that it would allow Maria to see her family and Alaric to have a grand time while he had to be away. We have a great community, one in which we support each other, so I knew I didn't have to be afraid to ask for assistance at different points throughout the hour. Something I have learned since moving to AZ and starting the program is that I have far more choice in making decisions or changing my perception than I initially might have believed. I do not have to take the option of a quiet life when there is so much I would like to do. Communication is an area I wish to develop, so I was thankful for this speaking opportunity and for those who showed up that day.

I decided to discuss this topic in two parts. When coming from the peace perspective, "Everything is impermanent" is an important consideration. Situations of imper-manence need not send us into a fearful panic; we can learn to view them with appreciation. Impermanence brings advances in technology that can help us achieve individual goals. Impermanence means growth, spiritually for ourselves, and physically for our children. (Who really wants their child to remain-an eight-month-old for their entire lifetime?) As a society we tend to view things negatively; thus, we automatically believe that impermanence equals suffering, when the suffering comes from not wanting things to change.

From the *Living Peace* perspective, and numerous other spiritual self-help volumes out there, we know we can always go back to our thoughts. Through a change in perception, what seems like a challenge can then become an opportunity.

The second part, "Change is the only constant"; that is, change is the only guarantee we have in life, is something that I now relish. Nonetheless, change is met by some with great fear and resistance. I would like to share with you this modern parable I found one day while browsing inspirational content on the Internet that illustrates the uselessness of such fear and resistance wonderfully:

The Parable of the Lobster

Long ago, when the world was very new, there was a certain lobster who was determined that the Creator had made a mistake. So he set up an appointment to discuss the matter.

"With all due respect," said the lobster, "I wish to complain about the way you designed my shell. You see, just as I get used to one outer casing, I have to shed it for another. Very inconvenient and rather a waste of time."

To which the Creator replied, "I see. But do you realize that it is the giving up of one shell that allows you to grow into another?"

"But I like myself just the way I am," the lobster said.

Your mind's made up?" the Creator asked.

"Indeed!" the lobster stated firmly.

"Very well," smiled the Creator. "From now on, your shell will not change, and you may go about your business just as you do right now."

"That's very kind of you," said the lobster and left.

At first, the lobster was very content wearing the same old shell. But as time passed, he found that his once light and comfortable shell was becoming quite heavy and tight.

After a while, in fact, the shell became so cumbersome that the lobster couldn't feel anything at all outside himself. As a result, he was constantly bumping into others.

Finally, it got to the point where he could hardly even breathe. So, with great effort, he went back to see the Creator.

"With all due respect," the lobster sighed, "contrary to what you promised, my shell has not remained the same; it keeps shrinking!"

"Not at all," smiled the Creator, "your shell may have gotten a little thicker with age, but it has remained the same size. What has happened is that you changed—inside, within your shell."

The Creator went on, "You see, everything changes continuously. No one remains the same. That's the way I've made things."

"That's very sensible," said lobster.

"If you like," offered the Creator, "I'll tell you something more."

"Please do," encouraged the lobster.

"When you let go of your shell and choose to grow," said the Creator, "you build new strength within yourself. And in that strength you'll find new capacity to love yourself... to love those around you... to love life itself. That is my plan for each of you."

http://pastorbriang.blogspot.com/2010/09/parable-of-lobster.html

(Edited from original by Shari Broyer)

So why are people inclined to feel fear when faced with change rather than embrace it? We have all been there, but it is worth examining this fear to remind ourselves of why we feel it and how we can best deal with change— should we choose to. Examining can lead to understanding.

Change has many unknowns which engender fear in us. The sense that we are losing control can often lead to feelings of anxiety. Fear of failure—and even fear of being successful—can hold us back. There is fear of what we may have to give up; fear of feeling uncomfortable; fear for our security; fear that others may judge, criticize or belittle us. Fear of being selfish, of letting others down... words like "should" and "must" then arise like specters to haunt us. Fear that we aren't capable, *ad infinitum*... We have so many options when choosing what to fear!

So, how do we overcome our fear of change?

A *Living Peace* perspective is Mastery of Thought: *"I think Peace... Mastering our thoughts can only be achieved after we truly understand what reality is... The majority of what you perceive as reality exists only in your mind, and chances are, you spend most hours of your life in this illusion. Let me repeat, if it didn't sink in the first time, the majority of what you perceive as reality exists only in your mind, and, chances are, you spend most hours of your life in this illusion."* ~ Alaric Hutchinson

I invite you to remember the only moment is the present, that's the only constant, ever-changing thing we have, so using tools to help us deal with "False Evidence Appearing Real" (FEAR) really helps ease our minds and keep us happily in the present instead of projecting our fears into a future that doesn't even exist.

At the other end of the scale of change, we find the saying, "Consider how hard it is to change yourself, and you'll understand what little chance you have of changing others."

I love this adage. It's a good reminder to focus on my own energetic vibration! When it comes to change, we can only change ourselves.

And so, I've now journeyed through the nine tenets, an exploration within, only to find myself back at the beginning, becoming aware of the thoughts I think in order to create my most peaceful, most joyous, and most loving reality possible. A true *Journey to Within* experience, one I hope you've enjoyed sharing with me.

I've included a summary of the Living Peace Tenets following this for those of you, who like me, know that this cycle and this journey, is continuous; review and relearning is all part of the process!

Summary of the
Living Peace Tenets

I MASTER MY THOUGHTS

Too often people forget to examine, check in with, or even question their beliefs. Do your beliefs feel good or do they bring you down all too often? What if I were to tell you that our beliefs are just thoughts? This is not new information, but it bears repeating. Beliefs have the power to limit you or empower you, so which thoughts do you prefer? Negative beliefs may appear very real and accurate, yet they can be changed so that they are uplifting.

Everything we think is perception, illusion. Take the example of a young child having a tantrum in the store. Some people might assume the child is badly behaved or the fact that the tantrum is occurring indicates a lack of good parenting skills. This is illusion—how do they know the cause? Perhaps there was a major change in the child's day, some trauma. Or, the child might be fitful due to lack of sleep, perhaps hungry, etcetera. Being open to understanding that there is always more going on than we are aware of allows us to release the thoughts and feelings about ourselves and others that might not feel so good.

If there is one piece of information that you take away from all that is written herein, I would invite you to explore your own thoughts and belief systems and see where they originate from. I like to keep things simple so I always examine my thoughts. I sit with them and acknowledge them before releasing or shifting them so that I may progress forward. It takes practice! At Earth Spirit Center for Healing we often refer to the "belief thief" concept. We are belief thieves when we pick up a thought from another and take it on as our own belief—ie. "I am not good enough" or "I can't do that." At the Center we actively work with looking at our thoughts and releasing the illusions created when we "steal" beliefs that do not serve our highest good.

I MASTER MY IMPULSES

Justifications and excuses are rife when it comes to not mastering our impulses. We can respond through Pause, Process and Respond/Retreat*. (*If we retreat to take a breather, we must come back and respond to, rather than ignore, an issue.)

First off: Pause... Breath is a **very** powerful, ever present, tool to turn to. When we are anxious, our breath becomes shallow and quick. Deliberately breathing slowly and deeply calms us down and assists with shifting our energy.

The Dunisha lifestyle encourages responding from a place of peace versus reacting, often negatively, to situations we do not like. When we do this, the experience tends to invite harmony in.

I MASTER MY EMOTIONS

The way to master our emotions is through persistence when dealing with our thoughts and impulses. There is no short cut around this! When we are dedicated to working with an awareness of our thoughts and impulses, we begin to experience a balanced emotional state. Over and over again, I've met people here in Arizona who are actively committed to their wellbeing and use these tenets and other tools to achieve it. It is beautiful and inspiring to witness.

However, it is also common to become attached to other people's stories and suffering in a way that is not good for them or ourselves. I am very fortunate that those I write to in prison have beautiful attitudes. I am aware that they do not share some of their hardest challenges with me. Though I am privy to this knowledge, I choose not to pity or look down upon them. Instead, I focus on penning uplifting, honest, heart-connected words. Not sweeping their reality away but holding it, to the best of my ability, in non-judgmental, loving, supportive space.

IGNORANCE IS AN ILLUSION, WE SEEK UNDERSTANDING

How many times have we been at the wrong end of someone's judgment of us, upset because we felt they didn't understand? How many times have *we* been the one to judge another in the same unthinking fashion?

It is not easy to gather every perspective or all information on every situation we encounter, so compassion is a great tool that helps us release our critical voices. I like to remind myself that we are all reflections of each other, thus my vibration is a direct consequence of how I view others.

It is also common for people to feel the need to tell others that they are "wrong" or somehow faulty for not living up to *their* standards and expectations. Compassion helps lead the way to acceptance and feeling better about ourselves and others since judging and being critical doesn't really do very much for us energetically.

CHAOS IS AN ILLUSION, WE SEEK HARMONY

It is a myth that peace is passive! Peace within is an active choice of being! We look through the eyes of someone living a Dunisha Lifestyle and see things as neither good nor bad. All things are just energetic vibrations.

Chaos comes about through misperception. When we take a step back from judgment and learn to be the calm within the center of a tornado, no matter how turbulent the external world seems, we experience inner harmony. Furthermore, when we change our internal "turmoil" of reacting, often the external "chaos" settles down.

We also allow. We allow other people to go through their own lives free from judgment, in a tolerant, loving, peaceful way. We allow them to be as they are.

DUALITY IS AN ILLUSION, WE SEEK TRANSCENDENCE

We seek to promote unity and peace by checking in with those perceptions. When we talk of "positive" we are asking ourselves, "Is this bringing hearts together?" or is it "negative", i.e.,"Is this isolating and separating humankind?" Unity is what we hold in our mind's eye. This tenet is one of my favorites. Having spent a decade corresponding with individuals in prison, I've learned so much about humankind via what they have shared with me.

WE RELEASE THE MUNDANE – THROUGH GRATITUDE AND TRUST

It is easy to get caught up with drama. *Everything is impermanent, change is always constant.* Knowing this, we can trust in the bigger picture. Life is like a pendulum. One moment all is well and we feel good, and then presto-chango! The pendulum swings the other way, and we feel challenged and totally fed up! Gratitude is the **Number One** tool we can use to direct us away from drama and out of suffering. I personally believe micro-focusing is most effective. When using a small lens, you're not comparing your fortune to another's, you're just exercising simple gratitude, such as "I have the skill of reading", "I have access to clean water", "I have a full toilet roll", or perhaps the choice of what to eat today or to live another day in physical form. When you're turning your focus so intently inward on what is good in YOUR life, you let go of the drama, both in your life and in the lives of others.

WE RELEASE KNOWING – THROUGH HUMILITY AND VULNERABILITY

The statement, "I know", is both a limitation and a cap on growth. Through keeping ourselves open by releasing judgments, expectations, etcetera, we allow further growth and wisdom in. We do this by being humble and seeing the best in all life. We allow ourselves to exercise vulnerability, to say, "I don't know." This is not a weakness since it allows us to let go of anything we are holding on to that may not be helpful for our all-round health.

WE RELEASE SELF – WE LET IT GO WITH LOVE

Through the wisdom of Dunisha living, when we refer to "ego" we mean the thoughts and actions that cause us to see others as separate from us in a negative way. We can each choose whether to view ourselves as separate or as ONE with another. The Dunisha perspective views separation from others as illusion. When a person knows securely who they are, the paradox of letting go of the self (ego) and embodying non-judgment and acceptance (inner peace), becomes a possible reality. Releasing labels that we have taken on from others (or put on ourselves) and further releasing our attachments to controlling life assists us in understanding that we are but one tiny part of the earth, and that there is a larger picture of humanity and the world. Releasing self opens us up to seeing the beauty all around us and allows further love to grow.

"To release ourselves, we must know ourselves, and that is when we gain the ability of authentic selfless service and the capacity for unconditional love." ~ Alaric Hutchinson

About the Author

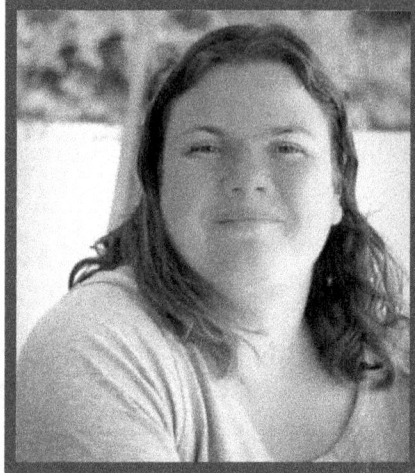

Born in the United Kingdom, Emma Porter has also lived and worked in Sweden, Singapore, and currently, the United States. With her love of travel and people, Emma's extensive international experiences and perspectives have served to enhance her peaceful lifestyle as a Dunisha Master.

Her passion is in finding practical ways to encourage people to believe that their emotional and spiritual well being matter, and she does this weekly at Earth Spirit Center for Healing in Arizona, where she resides with her two sons.

This is her first book.

www.ingramcontent.com/pod-product-compliance
Lightning Source LLC
Chambersburg PA
CBHW071017040426
42443CB00007B/812